I'M OFF
TO SEE
THE WIZARD

Brant Parker and Johnny Hart

A FAWCETT GOLD MEDAL BOOK

Fawcett Publications, Inc., Greenwich, Connecticut

I'M OFF TO SEE THE WIZARD

ISBN 0-449-13700-7

Printed in the United States of America

10 9 8 7 6 5 4 3 2

9-29

10-5

10-7

10-19

11-4

11-8

11-12

CRANK
CRANK
CRANK
CRANK
CRANK
CRANK
CRANK
CRANK
CRANK
CRANK
CRANK

12-4

12-18

12-29

12-30

January one ... nineteen seventy two

1-7

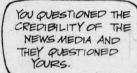

TOO MUCH SUN.

I THINK I'LL ENROLL IN A NIGHT COURSE.

2-7 ...IT'S IMPORTANT FOR A WIFE TO CONTINUE HER EDUCATION.

PLEASE LET IT BE SOMETHING TO DO WITH COOKING!

2-16

32

3·3

3-7

3-8

GREAT NEWS, SIRE!

...RODNEY WAS NAMED "MOST VALUABLE PLAYER" AT TODAY'S GAMES!

HOW SO?

HE WORE HIS DIAMOND SCABBARD.

WHAT'S IT LIKE OUTSIDE?

3-28

BLURRY.

YE GLASSE SHOPPE

HAND OVER ALL YOUR MONEY!

... AND IF I DON'T?

3-29

SHE HITS AN E ABOVE HIGH C.

4-3

4-5

WHY SO GLUM?

MY CLIENT WAS CONVICTED OF FORGERY.

OH, WELL... YOU WIN A FEW AND YOU LOSE A FEW....

ON THIS ONE, I LOST TWICE...

4-8

...HE PAID ME BY CHECK.

4-13

4-24

FOR YOUR **25 YEARS** OF **FAITHFUL SERVICE,** I PRESENT YOU WITH THIS CERTIFICATE, SIGNED BY THE **KING.**

5-1

THANK YOU! I'LL HAVE THIS FRAMED AND HANG IT, FOR **ALL OF MY FAMILY** TO SEE!

WHO HUNG THE CITATION OVER THE HALF MOON?

5-3

WE'RE TAKING A SURVEY...

...WHO DO **YOU** LIKE IN THE ELECTION?

5-9

THE SEEDY, LITTLE GUY THAT PAYS ME TO VOTE FOR THE KING.

5-22

OK, CY....HOLD THE CARD OVER ONE EYE..

NOW READ THE TOP LINE.

5-23

5-25

HEY CY,....WHAT'S HAPPENING MAN?

5-26

I LOST MY CONTACT LEN.

5-27

MORE MAGIC
FROM THE
WIZARD OF ID